AF255356

ticket
to
write

the teal one

r. m. s.

contents

introduction

2019 was, if you'll pardon my French, a *batshit insane* year.
There were not quite as many poems for me to choose from as in previous volumes, and some of them were written on tickets from airplanes and transcontinental railroads; these facts are related. I would like to be modest, but the fact you're holding an entire book that is exclusively full of random stuff I wrote means *that ship has sailed*, so: Ya girl got to intern at NASA. Did mean I was a tiny tad busy and not really taking buses, though.
The Usual Suspects, as the name implies, continue to help a lot with the collection of the tickets, and with ideas to fill them, and with maintaining my (increasingly) precarious sanity in the meantime:

- ♠ Mum, who has forgotten more about poetry than I'll ever know, and still somehow managed to read *all* the tickets without laughing or gagging or psychoanalyzing too enthusiastically;
- ♠ Dad, with whom I don't always have a language in common, but he tries to translate and I do notice and appreciate it, so this is an appendix to his glossary;
- ♠ M. of the dogs (p. 66), who gives me ideas above my station and for some peculiar reason seems to think I can make something of them;
- ♠ The Magnificent Sarah, with thanks for the cats and the mermaids and for being shrieked at in the middle of the day, which is the middle of the night, and vice versa;
- ♠ And the equally magnificent AJF, as ever, for all the usual reasons and a few more besides.

and so, without further ado...
ladies and gentlemen,
permit me to present you some poems.

I Don't Have Time
   To Trek Through This Again

One is concerned —
sometimes
to the point of fear —
in perpetuity:
that one will
miss something vital
or destroy it
or otherwise
epically fail.

A greater concern.
that one
already has
done all this failing
failed to do all this succeeding
& just
hasn't noticed yet —
that one day soon
this house of cards
will come crashing down
in a plume of dust
& thunder of tumbling concrete
The nervous whispered litany
one says to ward off this fear
a quickly — murmured list
of deeds well done
retains its virtue only till
the question rises
'yes but what's the point?'

i don't have time
to trek through this again

One is concerned –
sometimes
to the point of fear –
in perpetuity:
that one will
miss something vital
or destroy it
or otherwise
epically fail.
A greater concern:
that one
already has
done all this failing
failed to do all this succeeding
& just
hasn't noticed yet –
that one day soon
this house of cards
will come crashing down
in a plume of dust
& thunder of tumbling concrete.
The nervous whispered litany
one says to ward off this fear
(a quickly-murmured list
of deeds well done)
retains its little virtue
only until
the question rises
'yes, but what's the *point*?'

We don't have Coke;
is Pepsi okay?

I am
nobody's golden child
no straight-A-student poster-girl
no prodigy or protégée
or heroine or drug
I am
the middle-sized
philips-head screwdriver—
not perfectly sharpened
thoroughbred
to edge cases & precise work,
but clumsily adequate
for this, that, the other.
I am
the second-cheapest
instant coffee at the supermarket,
~~always~~ doing what
has to be done
sufficient in a pinch
(when you can't afford drip)
but without flair.
I am
tap water/printer paper/own-brand supp-
something you don't choose
to use —
merely mostly functional
until something better
becomes available.

```
www.busit.co.nz
Keep TKT for Inspectr

BUSIT!

Route 2
Driver:          11551
Ticket:           9481
Fare: UNI SV      $1.70
From
    96 Hillcrest Rd
To    Stop:17

Card: 145045
Credit Left: $6.00
Time: 19:02

14 Jan 19
** Transfer Expires **
8:02 PM

* free transfer trip *
*within city boundary*
*boarded before expiry*
** NOT TRANSFERABLE **

0800 4 BUSLINE
0800 4 2875463
```

we don't have coke; is pepsi okay?

I am
nobody's golden child
no straight-A-student poster-girl
no prodigy or protégée
or heroine or drug.
I am
the middle-sized
phillips-head screwdriver –
not perfectly sharpened,
thoroughbred
to edge cases & precise work,
but clumsily adequate
for this, that, the other.
I am
the second-cheapest
instant coffee at the supermarket –
doing what
has to be done,
sufficient in a pinch
(when you can't afford drip)
but without flair.
I am
tap water
printer paper
own-brand soap –
something you don't choose
to use
merely mostly functional
until something better
comes along.

Make a Wish / Thistle
Down

In the peak of summer,
when all her nobles are in
court,
you may see
Titania's people
going about their business
Sometimes they become
tangled in peasebloossom
snared by cobweb
If you
lift them up
gently clear away debris
& send them on their way
into the next breeze
with a whispered summary
of your heart's desire
When the tenth
or hundredth courier
rumbles safely home
reporting a new microdot
that weird kid   to
who wants to be
a rocket scientist'
Titania may nod & smile
& decide to stop your nagging
Be very careful therefore
how your desire is phrased

BUSIT!

Route 2
Driver: 10595
Ticket: 56
Fare: UNI SV $1.70
From Stop: 29

To   Stop: 25

Card: 145045
Credit Left: $2.60
Time: 17:29
24 Jan 19
** Transfer Expires **
6:29 PM

* Free transfer trip *
* within city boundary *
* boarded before expiry *
** NOT TRANSFERABLE **

0800 4 BUSLINE
0800 4 2875463

make a wish/thistle down

In the peak of summer,
when all her nobles are in court,
you may see
Titania's people
going about their business.
Sometimes they become
tangled in peaseblossom
snared by cobweb.
If you
lift them up
gently clear away detritus
& send them on their way
into the next breeze
with a whispered summary
of your heart's desire...
then when the tenth
or hundredth courtier
tumbles safely home
reporting a new fractional obligation,
Titania may nod & smile
& decided to stop your nagging.
Be very careful, therefore
how your desire is phrased.

```
      *** Not a  Valid ***
      ***     Ticket     ***
Driver                  11696
Module                 532141
Time                    07:01
Date      Thu. 07 Feb 19
      SmartCard Updated
Card:145045
Value Added:          $10.00
Card Cash Is:         $10.90
      *** Not a  Valid ***
      *** Travel Ticket ***
```

Vignette - Waiting

It is as if there were
a backyard
walled in
by high fences of yellow wood
No breeze blows here.
The air hangs
heavy
beaten by the sun
into leaden stillness
that resents every breath.
There are no flowers
Only crisply longdead grass
yellowed as a
desiccated corpse
So dry cracked packed earth
that breaks open at a touch
to pour through the fingers
like the remnants
of half-forgotten ambitions.

vignette: waiting

It is as if there were
a backyard,
walled in
by high fences of yellow wood.
No breeze blows here.
The air hangs
heavy,
beaten by the sun
into leaden stillness
that resents every breath.
There are no flowers;
only crisply longdead grass,
yellowed as a
desiccated corpse,
& dry cracked packed earth
that breaks open at a touch
to pour through the fingers
like the remnants
of half-forgotten ambitions.

Summertime, &
          Other Stories

These are
the glowing instants
 that you tuck away in envelopes
so that when the light is low
you can take them out
hold them up
keep the shadows at bay.
There is perhaps
sitting on a warm windowsill
very high up
watching a flaming sunset
with a good friend who is
singing you that song you like.
There is perhaps
The Fireworks Five Years Ago
locked in a mental snowglobe
sharper, more vivid & explosive
 with every repetition
than the real thing ever was.
Perhaps the emotional equivalent
of a tidal wave, as you realise
there are Larger Things
in the universe
than you can comprehend.
Perhaps a sleepy afternoon
watching snowflakes spiral down
to cover a skylight.
sometimes the envelope is even
almost full enough to assure you
that better times/ are not unprecedented

summertime, & other stories

These are
the glowing instants
that you tuck away in envelopes,
so that when the light is low
you can take them out,
hold them up,
keep the shadows at bay.
There is perhaps
sitting on a warm windowsill
very high up
watching a flaming sunset
with a good friend who is
singing you that song you like.
There is perhaps
the Fireworks Five Years Ago
locked in a mental snow-globe,
sharper, more vivid & explosive
with every repetition
than the real thing ever was.
Perhaps, the emotional equivalent
of a tidal wave, back when you realized
there are Larger Things
in the universe
than you can understand.
Perhaps a sleepy afternoon
watching snowflakes spiral down
to cover a skylight.
Sometimes the envelope is even
almost full enough to assure you
that better times
are not unprecedented.

May I have a soft-serve
        cone, please?
& it appears I have
what they call 'beer taste'
which are neither
discerning nor refined,
but here we go—
Fact
fast-food soft-serve is
the greatest dessert in the
                        world
A deliberate _invention_ not
like ice-cream proper
a discovery.
usually vanilla-flavor—
the 2nd-dearest spice of all
Pure white, aesthetically
.noffensive-to-pleasing
depending on swirl

Texture cohesive,
almost-stretchy, slight grit
so you know it's there
Slow-melting, well-shaping
until eaten, then
delectably liquid.
Come, Ganymede, purveyor
of ambrosia:
Swirl me your swirliest
soft-serve ice-cream-cone
Here is your fee — 70¢.

Route 2B
Driver: 11664
Ticket: 2674
Fare: UNI SV $1.70
From Stop:34

To   Stop:33

Card: 145045
Credit Left: $7.50
Time: 18:30
12 Feb 19
** Transfer Expires **
7:30 PM

* free transfer trip *
within city boundary
boarded before expiry
** NOT TRANSFERABLE **
WARNING.CARD VALUE LOW
0800 4 BUSLINE
0800 4 2875463

may i have a soft-serve cone, please?

& it appears I have
what they call 'beer tastes',
which are
neither discerning nor refined
but here we go.
Fact:
fast-food soft-serve is
the greatest dessert in the world.
A deliberate *invention*, not
like ice-cream proper
a discovery.
Usually vanilla-flavor –
the second-dearest spice of all.
Pure white, aesthetically
inoffensive-to-pleasing
depending on swirl.
Texture cohesive,
almost-stretchy, slight grit
so you know it's there.
Slow-melting, well-shaping,
until eaten, then
delectably liquid.
Come, Ganymede, purveyor
of ambrosia:
swirl me thy swirliest
soft-serve cone.
Here is thy fee: 70 ¢.

which is not really
              about doors

It has been
so long
in the house with
the stiff door-handles,
tugging hard
against old ratchet-gears,
sometimes just giving up
& going off to do something
useful.
but not
what you originally meant-
that when you move
unexpectedly
to another place
you have to take care
not to
wrench the handles off the doors;
not to
use too much force
now that things are
finally working properly

which is not really about doors

It has been
so long
in the house with
the stiff door-handles,
tugging hard
against old ratchet-gears,
sometimes just giving up
& going off to do something
useful
but not
what you originally meant –
that when you move
unexpectedly
to another place,
you have to take care
not to
wrench the handles off the doors,
not to
use too much force
now that things are
finally working properly.

Nightmares Are What
          You Make Them
It occurred
to my dream-self
the other night
to look up
in the middle of an idyll
when all the things
we never thought of wanting
(too impossible, too outlandish)
were there & real & happening
& she was happy &
not worrying or
carrying an ever-scrolling
to-do list in her head,
just living tranquil
with someone she adored
& worthy work.
But look up she did
& said
'You know
this is a nightmare,
right?'

nightmares are what you make them

It occurred
to my dream-self
the other night
to look up
in the middle of an idyll,
when all the things
we never thought of wanting
(too impossible, too outlandish)
were there & real & happening,
& she was happy &
not worrying or
carrying an ever-scrolling
to-do list in her head,
just living tranquil
with someone she adored
& doing worthy work.
But look up she did
& said
'You know
this is a nightmare,
right?'

The Big Wave

I always thought
it was a myth
or some
'super-spiritual' over-dramatic
SOB
being over-dramatic
or some
purely physiological/psychological
response to predictable stimuli.
& then one day
in a dim & silent corner
of a church
slowly emptying after the last hymn
the wave came.
& I stood
upside-down & inside-out
on the edge of a precipice
somewhere deep in the ocean;
swept off my feet close inshore
by tumbling surf
& brought here
breathing underwater
to meet God
At that precipice there is:
- the mindsucking personal insignificance
  of looking at a thousand
  other galaxies through the Hubble
  when your mind is barely big enough
  to understand the size of this one;
- the warm-blanket-on-cold-night
  center-of-the-universe feeling
  of someone loving specifically you
  quite a lot
  (I didn't recognize this one/until later)
- & peace so deep & profound & foreign
  it felt like chaos
- all multiplied x a few myriad
& now I know
in whom I have believed... &c.

the big wave

I always thought
it was a myth,
or some
'super-spiritual' over-dramatic SOB
being over-dramatic,
or some
purely physiological/psychological
response to predictable stimuli.
& then one day
in a dim & silent corner
of a church slowly emptying after the last hymn,
the wave came.
& I stood
upside-down & inside-out
on the edge of a precipice
somewhere deep in the ocean,
swept off my feet close inshore
by tumbling surf
& brought here, breathing underwater,
to meet God.
At that precipice there is:
- the mindsucking personal insignificance
  of looking at a thousand
  other galaxies through the Hubble
  when your mind is barely big enough
  to understand the size of this one;
- the warm-blanket-on-cold-night
  center-of-the-universe feeling
  of someone loving *specifically* you
  quite a lot
  (I didn't recognize this one until later)
- a peace so deep & profound & foreign
  it felt like chaos
- all multiplied × a few myriad.
 & now I know
 in whom I have believed... &c.

The Taste of Wanting

There used to be
Parma Violets —
pale purple
little pressed discs of powdered sugar
like pills.
You bought them in coin rolls
from the newsagent's
& they tasted
like the perfumed heart
of the blackest-purple violets
dipped in syrup
& nipped off between the teeth.
There used to be
long weeks of summer
hot & dry & sugar-sticky
until the black-purple clouds
unrolled
& the rain came down in sheets
& if you tilted back your head
to drink it in,
the shock of rain
sparkled in your mouth.
Somewhere between these two
is a faded-purple taste
that cloys & sparkles
& fills the whole body.
somewhere between these two
is a violet-perfumed flavor
with metallic glitter.
You find this ghost on your tongue
when you watch the shuttle taking off
near certain songs or otherwise
want some thing so badly/you can taste it.

the taste of wanting

There used to be
Parma Violets –
pale purple
little pressed discs of powdered sugar
like pills.
You bought them in coinrolls
from the newsagents
& they tasted
like the perfumed heart
of the black-purple violets
dipped in syrup
& nipped off between the teeth.
There used to be
long weeks of summer,
hot & dry & sugar-sticky
until the black-purple clouds
unrolled
& the rain came down in sheets
& if you tilted back your head
to drink it in,
the shock of rain
sparkled in your mouth.
Somewhere between these two
is a faded-purple taste
that cloys & sparkles
& fills the whole body.
Somewhere between these two
is a violet-perfumed flavor
with metallic glitter.
You find this ghost on your tongue
when you watch the Space Shuttle taking off or
hear certain songs or otherwise
want something so badly
you can taste it.

6 pm, Monday, Teaching
                Recess

& the silence
of the staffroom after hours —
when the coffee machine
is turned off
& the murmur of many
science-closed shoes
& voices
have wandered off —
is littered with
the little
unnoises
that create the soundscape
called
silence:
a clock ticks.
Cars sigh past on the road,
faintly heard
through thin elderly windows
& many yards of lawn.
The water boiler
grumbles occasionally.
Somewhere ~~through~~ beyond
many concrete walls, floors
a lab alarm
laments an intrusion.
In the perfect silence
that is unbroken only until
you stop to listen to it,
my own fingers,
gently releasing a coffee cup,
make a ~~little~~ musical chime.

6 pm, monday, teaching recess

& the silence
of the staffroom after hours –
when the coffee machine
is turned off
& the murmur of many
science-closed-shoes
& voices
has wandered off –
is littered with
the little
unnoises
that create the soundscape called
silence:
a clock ticks.
cars sigh past on the road,
faintly heard
through thin elderly windows
& over many yards of lawn.
the water boiler
grumbles occasionally.
Somewhere beyond
many concrete walls & floors,
a lab alarm
laments an intrusion.
In the perfect silence
that is unbroken only until
one stops to listen to it
my own fingers,
gently releasing a coffee cup,
make a crystalline musical chime.

In This Decade

Before 2029
they say
there will be
another human on the moon.
On the anarctic polar wastes
she will melt ice;
perhaps drink
for the first time in history
the water of
another world.
We choose
to go back to the moon
in this decade;
we choose
to have another generation stand
as their grandparents stood
downing tools
to cluster around a screen
& watch in awe
as another brave soul
takes another great leap
for all mankind.
And as for the other things?
we never really stopped
doing those.

in this decade

Before 2029
they say
there will be
another human on the moon.
On the anarctic polar wastes
she will melt ice;
perhaps drink
for the first time in history
the water of
another world.
We choose
to go back to the moon
in this decade;
we choose
to have another generation stand
as their grandparents stood
downing tools
to cluster around a screen
& watch in awe
as another brave soul
takes another great leap
for all mankind.
And as for the other things?
We never really stopped
doing those.
[a]

---

[a] Some possibly helpful context: *"But why, some say, the Moon? Why choose this as our goal? And they may well ask, why climb the highest mountain? Why, 35 years ago, fly the Atlantic? Why does Rice play Texas? We choose to go to the Moon!...We choose to go to the Moon in this decade and do the other things, not because they are easy, but because they are hard..."* – John F. Kennedy; Houston, Texas; September 12, 1962

There Will Be Death

& this will come
to an end
someday
in some way
as all good things do;
will join
the British Empire,
eight-track tapes,
Audrey Hepburn,
the convent on Clyde St,
& other great & terrible
weird & wonderful
earthly things that have passed away
leaving behind
only memories
& strange souvenirs –
the ashes
of an inferno that has burned its
There will be death.
There will be decay & loss
& things that feel like
the end of the f*****g world.

But the roses do not glow
less deep & vivid
in the sunlight
of late summer;
the grass is not less
rich electric green
under the willows;
just because they know
it will rain tomorrow.

www.busit.co.nz
Keep TKT for Inspectr

BUSIT!

Route 9
Driver: 11789
Ticket: 4683
Fare: UNI SV $1.70
From Stop:11

To   Stop:10

Card: 145045
Credit Left: $0.50
Time: 18:39
04 May 19
** Transfer Expires **
7:39 PM

* Free transfer trip *
within city boundary
boarded before expiry
** NOT TRANSFERABLE **
WARNING, CARD VALUE LOW

0800 4 BUSLINE
0800 4 2875463

there will be death

& this will come
to an end
someday
in some way
as all good things do.
It will join
the British Empire,
eight-track tapes,
Audrey Hepburn,
the convent on Clyde Street,
& other great & terrible,
weird & wonderful
earthly things that have passed away,
leaving behind
only memories
& strange souvenirs:
the ashes
of an inferno that has burned its course.
There will be death.
There will be decay
& loss
& things that feel like
the end of the f*****g world.
But the roses do not glow
less deep & vivid
in the sunlight
of late summer;
the grass is not less
rich electric green
under the willows;
just because they know
it will rain tomorrow.

WANTED ON VOYAGE –
   THIS WAY UP

& because
I have to go soon –
halfway
around the world in fact
I need my head turned
the right way up :-
so all the
to-do lists
flight numbers
job details
do not fall out.
But soon is not now
& for now
I can tilt it over enough
to rest on your shoulder
& fall asleep
without anything too vital
shaking loose.
Wake me up
when they call economy
or
for the heat-death of the universe.
I'll want to see that.

AIR NEW ZEALAND

A STAR ALLIANCE MEMBER

SEAT
5813
03C

& because
I have to go soon –
halfway
around the world in fact –
I need my head turned
the right way up:
so all the
to-do lists
flight numbers
job details
do not fall out.
But *soon* is not *now*
& for now
I can tilt it over enough
to rest on your shoulder
& fall asleep
without anything too vital
shaking loose.
Wake me up
when they call economy
or
for the heat-death of the universe.
I'll want to see that.

FLIGHT: NZ5813
FROM: **HLZ**   TO: **WLG**
DATE: **13MAY**

ESTIMATED
BOARDING: **07:35**AM

SEAT: **03C**

The Seatbelt Sign is Illuminated

Today (most days) I am
the impecunious speed-demon
getting high on
the wind in my hair
the acceleration
showing me jealously
 but ineffectually
back in my seat.
No needle tracks for this drug.
No brakes either.
The ultimate of course is
take-off in a small aeroplane —
going faster & faster until
the earth itself cannot hold me.
Next challenge: restraining the urge
to laugh as high-maniacally as I felt
 when the wheels leave the ground.

the seatbelt sign is illuminated

Today (most days) I am
The impecunious speed-demon
getting high on
the wind in my hair
the acceleration
shoving me jealously
but ineffectually
back in my seat.
No needle tracks for this drug.
No brakes either.
The ultimate of course is
take-off in a small aeroplane –
going faster & faster until
the earth itself cannot hold me.
Next challenge:
restraining the urge
to laugh as high-maniacally as I feel
when the wheels leave the ground.

Dawn Comes Early at 17,000 ft.

It is a stormy morning
down there -
the edges of the bay
are marked with the
surging swells of lightfoam -
a wave of headlights -
early commuters.
In the flat-plain steppes
of cloud country,
we scream through the air
& the little hills on the horizon
keep pace,
serenely still
against the eternally red sky
of a long-drawn dawn.
Under the waves,
in the occasional pits between
airy whitecaps -
deep, very deep,
glows Atlantis.

dawn comes early at 17,000 ft

It is a stormy morning
down there –
the edges of the bay
are marked with the
surging swells of lightfoam –
a wave of headlights –
early commuters.
In the flat-plain steppes
of cloud country,
we scream through the air
& the little hills on the horizon
keep pace,
serenely still
against the eternally red sky
of a long-drawn dawn.
Under the waves,
in the occasional pits between
airy whitecaps –
deep, very deep,
glows Atlantis.

```
FLIGHT:        NZ5810
FROM: WLG   TO: HLZ
DATE:          14MAY

ESTIMATED
BOARDING:      06:00AM


SEAT:          06C
                KA13
```

Localized Time-Warp

Look at your watch.
Now back at me.
We shall conduct an experiment [to test
a lesser-known
principle of relativity:
that time speeds up
when you (an observer) are
having fun or
~~time~~ close to someone you love ^[very much] or
when you don't have much left.
Time flees like a startled blackbird fo
the moments you wanted most
to last forever.
Now back at your watch.
It's been an hour. Science, man.

localized time-warp

Look at your watch.
Now look back up.
We shall conduct an experiment to test
a lesser-known
principle of relativity:
that time speeds up
when you (an observer) are
having fun or
close to someone you love very much or
when you don't have much left.
Time flees like a startled blackbird from
the moments you wanted most
to last forever.
When you look back at your watch,
it's been an hour.
Science, man.

I Will Almost Miss the Rain

when the storm clouds
well black &
the night
comes at noon over the hill
while the sun
still pours down
behind the wall
in the city;
when the ducks
shake themselves busily
out of their naps
on the muddy bank
& go to work
splashing in the puddles
polishing
their iridescent feathers;
when little rivers
run in the gutters,
washing away
the accumulated grime;
when the dry soil
drinks deeply,
in little sighing sips
& the heads of the grass
are bowed under
the weight of diamonds;
then Hamilton is lovely
& then

i will almost miss the rain

When the storm clouds
well black &
the night
comes at noon over the hills
while the sun
still pours down
behind the wall
in the city;
when the ducks
shake themselves busily
out of their naps
on the muddy bank
& go to work,
splashing in the puddles,
polishing
their iridescent feathers;
when little rivers
run in the gutters,
washing away
the accumulated grime;
when the dry soil
drinks deeply
in little sighing sips
& the heads of the grass
are bowed under
the weight of diamonds;
then Hamilton is lovely
& then
I will almost miss the rain.

Cthulhages

& his reaching fingers
loom out of the darkness
in the depths of the printed rocket nozzle
for if you joke about him
too loudly
the trees of the print
will be decayed
& the cthulhages come looking
for over-talkative engineers.
& his staring eyes
bore gummy holes
in the surface of a cake
for if you say his name
too often
the bubbles in the batter
will boil up
& the cthulhages peer through
to see if you have
that cartoon about cthulhulation of the sea
in your kitchen.
Be careful, then
where you are when you speak R'lyeh
& move the stones in the pond gently
& wipe away the cobwebs softly
for Cthulhu's slumber is uneasy in the ocean
& his sleeping eyes watch on.

cthulhages

& his reaching fingers
loom out of the darkness
of the depths of the printed rocket-nozzle
for if you joke about him
too loudly
the trees of the print
will be decayed
& the Cthulhages come looking
for over-talkative engineers.
& his staring eyes
bore gummy holes
in the surface of a cake
for if you say his name
too often
the bubbles in the batter
will boil up
& the Cthulhages peer through
to see if you have
that cartoon about the Cthulhulation of the seas
in your kitchen.
Be careful, then,
where you are when you speak R'lyeh,
& move the stones in the pond gently,
& wipe away the cobwebs softly,
for Cthulhu's slumber is uneasy in the ocean
& his sleeping eyes watch on.

БЛОГ/ВЛОГ/backspace

I can
look pleasantly at the camera,
keep all the words
in my head
or say them
in the right order,
maybe two of these,
not all three.
If I make a typo here
I cannot back the cursor up
& fix just one second
seamlessly-
mistakes require do-overs.
what's past is locked
on film
read-only,
& sometimes (often)
'sorry, I'll do
that again'
is not enough
does not erase
what came before.
& in this single
reel of film that's life,
whoops, I meant to say
means less
than what was said.

блог/влог/бекспейс (blog/ vlog/ backspace)

I can
look pleasantly at the camera,
keep all the words
in my head,
or say them
in the right order;
maybe two of these;
not all three.
If I make a typo here
I cannot back the cursor off
& fix just one second
seamlessly.
Mistakes require do-overs.
What's past is locked
on film
read-only
& sometimes (often)
'sorry I'll do
that again'
is not enough
does not erase
what came before.
& in this single
reel of film that's life,
'whoops I *meant* to say'
means less
than what was said.[a]

---

[a] Written sometime in summer, in Mountain View, CA.

Keep TKT for Inspector

BUSIT!

*** Not a Valid ***
***   Ticket   ***

Driver   10394
Module   522780
Time   08:36
Date   Sun, 19 May 19
     SmartCard Updated
Card:145045
Value Added: $10.00
Card Cash Is: $10.50
  *** Not a Valid ***
  *** Travel Ticket ***

Thoughts of 'Home' on the
Stevens Creek Trail.

Here I am
walking beside the creek
that runs in a culvert
& there are
blackberries
holding out
long grasping fingers
with sharp nails
as if to say
'come, taste'
'remember
the place you call home'
'remember
a different place
that felt like home'.
& so at their bidding
I reach out
through the thorns
to the rich dark cluster of
a ripe blackberry among the flowers
Hold it for a minute. Decide.
It has the sweet purple
metallic taste/of wanting.

thoughts of 'home' on the stevens creek trail

Here I am
walking beside the creek
that runs in a culvert
& there are
blackberries
holding out
long grasping fingers
with sharp nails
as if to say
'come, taste';
'remember
the place you call home';
'remember
a different place
that felt like home';
& so at their bidding
I reach out
through the thorns
to the rich dark cluster of
a ripe blackberry among the flowers.
Hold it for a minute.
Decide.
It has the sweet-purple
metallic taste
of wanting.[a]

---

[a] Written sometime in summer, in Mountain View, CA.

The Queen Anne's lace is yellow here
a disorderly crowd of flat-topped blondes
straggling up the railway bank
trying to look like a rapeseed field in spring
& not doing very well at it.

I had not seen
an all-out desert before — life so far has been
green, ocean-lined, never too far
from crashing wave or rainy day.
This flat, dead, sandy plain
glares sullenly up: Here I am,
hurry through, or stay forever.

I can see why people
choose to be here —
the red rocks coat themselves
in heavy green fir
& present a friendlier face to cañons & canoes
& the mountains leap a mile in the sky
& look almost like home.

God is wise — for lo, They have provided
unto all in the middle of a continent
who will never see the flat sharp blade
of an ocean horizon
the flat sharp blade of the horizon
in an ocean of level corn fields

To see West Virginia at long last with my own eyes
after so many years hearing John Denver
is a kind of para-homecoming; it is not my home
but it is somebody's, not just another place
& so I try to look on it with respect.

coast-to-coast amtrak

The Queen Anne's Lace is yellowed here
a disorderly crowd of flat-topped blondes
straggling up the railway bank
trying to look like a rapeseed field in spring
& not doing very well at it.

____

I had not seen
an all-out desert before – life so far has been
green, ocean-lined, never too far
from crashing waves or rainy days.
This flat, dead, sandy plain
glares sullenly up: here I am.
Hurry through or stay forever.

____

I can see why people
choose to be here –
the red rocks coat themselves
in heavy green fir
& present a friendlier face to cañons & canoes
& the mountains leap a mile in the sky
& almost look like home.

____

God is wise – for lo, He has provided
to the middle of a continent
who will never see the flat sharp blade
of an ocean horizon
the flat sharp blade of the horizon
in an ocean of level cornfields.

____

To see West Virginia at long last with my own eyes
after so many years hearing John Denver
is a kind of para-homecoming: it is not my home
but it is somebody's.
Not just another place.
& so I try to look on it with respect.

Cold

They say; never
go back to a place
(or is it
you _can_
~~never~~
go back to a place?
the latter would be true
due to dimensional constr
the former...)
I've done it twice now.
& the place
has changed
& it still feels strange
because the little changes
a shop here
a signpost there
a moved bus stop —
changes
Monet would not catch —
stack up
& unless you manage
to spot them all
it is
a return to 2001
where everything is
just the way you'd expect
it to be
but ever so slightly
off.
& I am not sure when I will
                        get to

```
www.busit.co.nz
Keep TKT for Inspectr
- - - - - - - - - - - - - - - -

┌────────────────────┐
│     BUSIT!         │
└────────────────────┘

Route 9B
Driver:          11723
Ticket:           1705
Fare: UNI SV      $1.70
From Stop:25

To    Stop:24

Card: 145045
Credit Left: $3.70
Time: 06:59
     28 Aug 19
** Transfer Expires **
     07:59 AM

* Free transfer trip *
*within city boundary*
*boarded before expiry*
** NOT TRANSFERABLE **

0800 4 BUSLINE
0800 4 2875463
```

They say, never
go back to a place
(or is it
you can
never
go back to a place?
The latter would be true,
due to dimensional constraints,
the former...)
I've done it twice now.
& the place
has changed
& it still feels strange
because the little changes –
a shop here,
a signpost there,
a moved bus stop –
changes
Monet would not catch –
stack up
& unless you manage
to spot them all
it is
a return to 2001
where everything is
just the way you'd expect
but ever so slightly
off.
& I am not sure
when I will get home.

On The Beach

& the rain
arrives in ribbons
over the shimmering surface
of the water
like the stripes
of fingers
dragged across a suede couch.

the waves crash
on the steep shore
un naturally narrow
unnaturally yellow
at the steep concrete cliff
& the spray dashes
against the coats
of the people who stand
waiting for the boats.
The arks
come & go
grating aground on the beach
& push off again
chassis
scraping across the R
yellow paint
on the kerb,
wheels splashing through
the thin film of water
on the concrete apron
of the bus depot.

on the beach

& the rain
arrives in ribbons
over the shimmering surface
of the water,
like the stripes
of fingers
dragged across a suede couch.
The waves crash
on the shore,
unnaturally narrow,
unnaturally yellow,
at the steep concrete cliff
& the spray dashes
against the coats
of the people who stand
waiting for the boats.
The arks
come & go,
grating aground on the beach
& pushing off again,
chassis
scraping across the yellow paint
on the curb,
wheels splashing through
the thin film of water
on the concrete apron
of the bus depot.

The
Love & Other Drugs Album
(Track 1)

& I have
altered my mind before now
— what intelligent
bored
wannabe-unconventional
pretentious-poetry-writing
seeker-type
hasn't?
My ~~nastixin~~
~~salvia~~
~~nicotine~~
~~ethanol~~ — .
okay.
nothing illegal
expensive
long-lasting
life-changing
smart, right?
seeking out
the ever smoother calm
& higher high
with no strings attached.
makes sense that I
would end up here.
I finally found
a high I don't want
to come down from.
(Just as well; not sure I can.)

love & other drugs (track 1)

& I have
altered my mind before now:
what intelligent
bored
wannabe-unconventional
pretentious-poetry-writing
seeker-type
hasn't?
Myristicin
salvia
nicotine
ethanol –
okay.
Nothing illegal
expensive
long-lasting
life-changing
smart, right?
Seeking out
the ever-smoother calm
& ever-higher high
with no strings attached.
Makes sense that I
would end up here.
I finally found
a high I don't want
to come down from.
(Just as well;
not sure I can.)

Love & Other Drugs
  (Track 2)
I am not high anymore
so that's something.
It was a long trip home
& for two years now
my life has been
in orbit
waiting for
that one little extra thrust
to get the hell away
from this town
out of Dodge
on a one-way train
going anywhere.
Perhaps I am high
on something less concrete
after all
because I find myself
seriously imagining
staying.

love & other drugs (track 2)

I am not high anymore
so that's something.
It was a long trip home
& for two years now
my life has been
in orbit
waiting for
that one little extra thrust
to get the hell away
from this town
out of Dodge
on a one-way train
going anywhere.
Perhaps I am hooked
on something less concrete
after all
because I find myself
seriously considering
staying.

We are off the Yellow Brick Road
& into the Poppy Fields

I have no concept
of twenty years
ten years
as a plannable chunk of time.
I would like to
– be that grownup
  who shrugs & says
  'but that was
   a very long time ago'
  & means it.
– still be in touch
  with people
  from ten-fifteen
  years ago
  & not just hate-read
   their blogs.
 – have a career
  all planned out
  more than
  a 'meh' and a handwave
  at least to within
  the nearest continent
  is that
  too much to ask?
But in ten years
a lot of random windfalls
million-to-one odds
& freak accidents
can occur
& I guess if I wanted
to ignore all of them
I could make some kind of plan

we are off the yellow brick road & into the poppy fields

I have no concept
of twenty years
(or ten years)
as a plannable chunk of time.
I would like to
- be that grownup
   who shrugs & says
   'but that was
   a very long time ago'
   & means it.
- still be in touch
   with people
   from ten-fifteen years ago
   & not just hate-read
   their blogs.
- have a career
   all planned out
   more than
   a 'meh' and a handwave
   at least to within
   the nearest continent
   is that too much to ask?
But in ten years
a lot of random windfalls
million-to-one odds
& freak accidents
can occur
& I guess if I wanted
to ignore *all* of them
I could make
some kind of plan.

O.L.O. here & now

Hail, Mary, full of grace;
I wonder if you're listening.
I wonder if you recognise her.
the pale
tranquil
melancholy
centerpiece of many shrines
obverse detail of many medallions
revered object of many icons?
The LORD is with thee;
& with me;
They said so.
Blessed art thou among women
& blessed is
the fruit of thy womb
Jesus.
I wonder if he recognizes
himself in the pictures.
Does he mind (do you?)
being drawn
Korean
Spanish
British
Eritrean
maori?
Holy Mary, Mother of God,
how does it feel to be so right-
eous
that your prayers are
more effective than the Pope's?
Pray for me, Mary; please
ask God to tell me what They
want.

our lady of here & now

Hail Mary, full of grace,
I wonder if you're listening.
I wonder if you recognize her,
the pale
tranquil
melancholy
centerpiece of many shrines
obverse detail of many medallions
revered object of many icons?
The LORD is with thee;
& with me;
He said so.
Blessed art thou among women
& blessed is
the fruit of thy womb
Jesus.
I wonder if he recognizes
himself in the pictures.
Does he mind (do you?)
being drawn
Korean
Spanish
British
Eritrean
Māori?
Holy Mary, Mother of God,
how does it feel to be so righteous
that your prayers are
more effective than the Pope's?
Pray for me, Mary: please
ask God to tell me
what He wants.

The Original Green
(no reprise)

& the grass is
always greener
& the water
always cleaner

& the waves
crawl softer
up upon
the shores I've left behind.
A wise man said
that if you go
with gaze turned back
to what you know
it won't be very long before
your path becomes
a wall.

& Voyager
will not return;
it wouldn't find
where it had been,
but only what
the earth is now:
that's not the same
at all.
& as I ride along the rail
of missions done & missions failed
(each far horizon
(back & forward)
glows the Original Green.

the original green (no reprise)

& the grass is
always greener
& the water
always cleaner
& the waves
crawl softer
up upon
the shores I've left behind.
A wise man said
that if you go
with gaze turned back
to what you know
it won't be very long before
your path becomes
a wall.
& Voyager
will not return:
it wouldn't find
where it had been,
but only what
the Earth is now.
That's not the same
at all.

I want (Mark 10:29-31)

The things I leave behind
in your name, o God,
you say you will
pay me back 100 times
eventually.
The trouble is, Lord,
telling me you will replace
something unique
something irreplaceable
something you totally can
(but probably won't)
save for me
or for its own sake
or Just Frickin' Because
It's worth saving
anyway: that's a lie.
I don't want a hundred.
I want this one.
Is that too much to ask?
And you who are reading
waiting for
a neat resolution
a saintly Acceptance —
well, you're not
going to get one.
Because this sucks
& I don't understand.

www.busit.co.nz
Keep TKT for Inspectr

BUSIT!

Route 52A
    Driver: 11685
    Ticket: 273
Fare: UNI SV $1.70
From Stop:6

To   Stop:7

Card: 145045
Credit Left: $8.20
Time: 09:27
22 Sep 19
** Transfer Expires **
10:27 AM

* Free transfer trip *
within city boundary
boarded before expiry
** NOT TRANSFERABLE **

0800 4 BUSLINE
0800 4 2875463

i want (mark 10:29–31)

The things I leave behind
in your name, O God,
you say you will
pay me back a hundred times
eventually.
The trouble is, LORD,
telling me you will replace
something unique
something irreplaceable
something you totally can
(but probably won't)
save for me
or for its own sake
or Just Frickin' Because
It's Worth Saving:
that's a lie.
I don't want a hundred.
I want this one.
Is that too much to ask?
And you who are reading
waiting for
a neat resolution
a saintly Acceptance –
well, you're not
going to get one.
Because this sucks
& I don't understand.

Hope

They say
when God wants to punish you
They will give you
what you asked for.
& here we are:
I have it all.
Science, literature,
mild notoreity,
conferences, panels,
papers, true love (?),
groundbreaking research,
a job I like,
broad interests, travel,
fulfilling hobbies... (about
& I never really thought

how hard it is
to balance
how neurotic
& stubborn
& tireless
you have to be
& how fast you reach
the limit
of tolerance —
the point at which
you cannot sanely survive
getting
what you asked for.

www.busit.co.nz
Keep Tkt for Inspectr

BUSIT!

Route 9B
Driver: 11723
Ticket: 7693
Fare: UNI SV $1.70
From Stop:25

To   Stop:24

Card: 145045
Credit Left: $3.10
Time: 06:58
      09 Oct 19
** Transfer Expires **
      07:58 AM

* Free transfer trip *
within city boundary
boarded before expiry
** NOT TRANSFERABLE **

0800 4 BUSLINE
0800 4 2875463

hope

It is said
when God wants to punish you
He will give you
what you asked for.
& here we are:
I have it all.
Science, literature,
mild notoriety,
conferences, panels, papers,
groundbreaking research,
a job I like,
broad interests, travel,
fulfilling hobbies...
& I never really thought about
how hard it is
to balance;
how neurotic
& stubborn
& tireless
you have to be
& how fast you reach
the limit
of tolerance –
the point at which
you cannot sanely survive
getting
what you asked for.

Urban Forest
~~Jungle~~

except in Auckland
(which is
a different country
& doesn't count)
there is not
urban jungle here –
with tall thick-trunked
steel-&-glass trees;
undergrowth of
stop signs, store canopies,
bus shelters, kiosks;
heavy cable vines.

They tell us we shall have
instead
a patchwork blanket
bits of forest (with real trees)
scattered across
the asphalt
urban desert

www.busit.co.nz
Keep TKT for Inspectr

*** Not a Valid ***
***   Ticket   ***
Driver   11723
Module   548320
Time   06:59
Date   Mon. 14 Oct 19
    SmartCard Updated
Card:145045
Value Added: $10.00
Card Cash Is: $11.40
 *** Not a Valid ***
 *** Travel Ticket ***

urban forest, urban jungle

except in Auckland
(which is
a different country
& doesn't count)
there is not
urban jungle here;
with tall thick-trunked
steel-&-glass trees;
undergrowth of
stop signs, store canopies,
bus shelters, kiosks;
heavy cable vines.
They tell us we shall have
instead
a patchwork blanket
bits of forest (with real trees)
scattered across
the asphalt
urban desert.

There are Mermaids
   on Enceladus
There is room
in this very serious
very grown-up field
where we are all
doing very important things
that make the world
infinitessimally better (we hope)
to make jokes about mermaids
in project titles —
to stop & pat the dogs
in between recording data
about them —
to cackle hysterically about
how your thesis research
is literal bullshit —
to make candy
in the lab —
to go on overdramatic
Expeditions
to recapture escaped bees.
In the relative privacy
of the laboratory
or the mixed-faculty tearoom
quite a lot of
these boring, scary, weird,
obsessive scientists
have something resembling
a sense of humor.

BUSIT!

Route 9B
Driver: 11723
Ticket: 8130
Fare: UNI SV $1.70
From Stop: 25

To   Stop: 24

Card: 145045
Credit Left: $9.70
Time: 06:59
   14 Oct 19
** Transfer Expires **
   07:59 AM

* free transfer trip *
* within city boundary *
* boarded before expiry *
** NOT TRANSFERABLE **

0800 4 BUSLINE
0800 4 2875463

there are mermaids on enceladus

There is room
in this very serious
very grown-up field
where we are all
doing very important things
that daily make the world
infinitesimally better (we hope);
to make jokes about mermaids
in project titles[a] –
to stop & pat the dogs
in between recording data
about them[b] –
to laugh hysterically about
how your thesis research
is literal bullshit[c] –
to make candy
in the lab[d] –
to go on overdramatic
Expeditions
to recapture escaped bees[e].
In the relative privacy
of the laboratory
or the mixed-faculty tearoom
quite a lot of
these boring, scary, weird, obsessive scientists
have something resembling
a sense of humor.

---

[a] Project ARIELLE is about looking for life on oceanic moons of outer planets.
[b] M.'s research is about canine scent-detection training.
[c] F.'s research is about the effects of dung-beetle biomass and relative size on their efficiency in subsuming cow manure.
[d] R.'s research is about the potential health benefits of some honey that tastes bad but makes passable toffee.
[e] N. was looking at the trace element profiles of bees' brains.

Heretic/Disciple

There is a certain molecule
(that I only know about
    because a friend
    is really into all this)
& some people
write important papers saying
it behaves in a curve
& other people
equally clever & qualified
write equally important papers saying
it behaves in a straight line.
This is a crucial distinction
to all the people
who care about the molecule.
This distinction
is worth
millions of dollars
dozens of jobs so far
& hundreds of papers
around the world
saying in polite academic
'hey f*ckwit you're wrong.'
To the people
who care about the molecule
it is jobs/lives/reputations
made & ruined.
To outsiders, the two factions
of the church of the molecule
are indistinguishable.

```
Route 52
  Driver:           11763
  Ticket:            3324
Fare: UNI SV        $1.70
From Stop:1

To    Stop:2

Card: 145045
Credit Left: $8.00
Time: 19:10
    14 Oct 19
** Transfer Expires **
    8:10 PM

*  free transfer trip  *
* within city boundary *
* boarded before expiry*
**  NOT TRANSFERABLE  **

0800 4 BUSLINE
0800 4 2875463
```

heretic/disciple

There is a certain molecule
(that I only know about
because a friend
is really into all this)
& some people
write important papers saying
it behaves in a curve;
& other people,
equally clever & qualified,
write equally important papers saying
it behaves in a straight line.
This is a crucial distinction
to all the people
who care about the molecule.
This distinction
is worth
millions of dollars
dozens of jobs so far
& hundreds of papers
around the world
saying in polite Academic
'hey moron you're wrong'.
To the people
who care about the molecule,
it is jobs
lives
reputations
made & ruined.
To outsiders, the two factions
of the church of the molecule
are indistinguishable.

2012

The world was
supposed to end.
All those ancient calendars
just stop
around Christmas
2012.
Is this a sign of loss-of-faith
a calm belief
the world would cease to be
at some time
lost in the grey mist
of that-which-is-to-come
& so
unimportant
except to remember
to stop writing the calendar?
Or is it faith in action
the pedestrian hope
that in the distant year
2012
there would still be
humans
civilization
chronologists
ready to continue?
Is it this same hope
that cuts off cellphone
calendars
at 2100?

Keep TKT for Inspect

BUSIT!

Route 13
Driver: 11638
Ticket: 4265
Fare:UNI SV $1.70
From Stop:25

To   Stop:24

Card: 145045
Credit Left: $6.30
Time: 18:34
22 Oct 19
** Transfer Expires **
7:34 PM

Free transfer trip
within city boundary
boarded before expiry
** NOT TRANSFERABLE **

0800 4 BUSLINE
0800 4 2875463

2012

The world was
supposed to end.
All those ancient calendars
just stop
around Christmas
2012.
Was this a sign of loss-of-faith?
a calm belief
the world would cease to be
at some time
lost in the grey mist
of that-which-is-to-come
& so
unimportant
except to remember
to stop writing the calendar?
Or is it faith in action
the pedestrian hope
that in the distant year
2012
there would still be
humans
civilization
chronologists
ready to continue?
Is it this same hope
that cuts off
cellphone calendars
at 2100?

After 2012
The world was
supposed to end.
Perhaps it did.
can you really say –
can I
it has all been the same
since then?
Was 2012 not
the year it all
changed?
For me, I
went halfway around the world
to a place
where the people who knew
they belonged there
looked like me.
I grew up there, I think,
because
since then,
everything has been
the denouement
of a murder-mystery:
where little things long ago
fall inevitably together
without being touched
to form a cohesive whole
so the plot makes
an alien kind of sense

www.busit.co.nz
Keep IKT for Inspector

BUS IT!

written 25/10/19 AM
Route 2
Driver: 11572
Ticket: 374
Fare: UNI SV $1.70
From Stop: 24

To   Stop: 23

Card: 145045
Credit Left: $5.20
Time: 18:02
30 Aug 19
** Transfer Expires **
7:02 PM

* Free transfer trip *
* within city boundary *
* boarded before expiry *
* NOT TRANSFERABLE *

0800 4 BUSLINE
0800 4 2875463

after 2012

The world was
supposed to end.
Perhaps it did.
Can you really say –
can I –
it has all been the same
since then?
Was 2012 not
the year it all
changed?
For me, I
went halfway around the world
to a place
where the people
who knew they belonged there
looked like me.
I grew up there, I think,
because
since then,
everything has been
the denouement
of a murder-mystery:
where little things long ago
fall inevitably together,
without being touched,
to form a cohesive whole
so the plot makes
an alien kind of sense.

From The Center
  To The Edges

I remember
an immersive painting
I saw in San Jose.
It walked on air
on a crisp cold pastel morning
& pulled the gallery with it
into the pale dawn ghost
of anonymous mountains
unlike & like
mountains any living eye
has ever seen.
I remember
standing in the air bakery
just off the fourth floor
of the library
 on a crisp cold pastel morning
with the pale dawn ghost
of the world
pulling me with it into
mountains no living eye
has ever seen.
I remember
the crisp pale taste of nitrogen.
I remember
that as long as
the pull of the edges
is there as a refuge
I can stay in the center.

from the center to the edges

I remember
an immersive painting
I saw in San Jose.
It walked on air
on a crisp cold pastel morning
& pulled the gallery with it
into the pale dawn ghost
of anonymous mountains
unlike & like
any mountains any living eye
has ever seen.
I remember
standing in the air
just off the fourth-floor balcony
of the library
on a crisp cold pastel morning
with the pale dawn ghost
of the world
pulling me with it into
mountains no living eye
has ever seen.
I remember
the crisp pale taste of nitrogen.
I remember
that as long as
the pull of the edges
is there as a refuge
I can stay in the center. [a]

---

[a] Title refers to Kathryn Metz's work of the same name, which was shown at
the Triton Museum of Art in Santa Clara between May 11 & August 18, 2019

Loser

'I can't do it', I say
as I go about doing it.
'This will never work', I say
as it does.
'I'm sure I failed', I say
moments before opening
a straight-A transcript.
I know it annoys you.
I know that passing is
technically enough &
why can't I just be
satisfied with that?
But yet again
we are not seeing
the same world.
I watch as everyone else
seems to muddle by
well enough
unfailingly okay
at everything they try to do
while I work so hard
just to break down
my own perfectionism enough
to open the Word document
start typing.
Because when 'good enough' is not
mediocrity is not better than
nothing

loser

"I can't do it", I say
as I go about doing it.
"This will never work," I say
as it does.
"I'm sure I failed," I say
moments before opening
a straight-A transcript.
I know it annoys you.
I know that passing is
technically enough &
why can't I just be
satisfied with that?
But yet again
we are not seeing
the same world.
I watch as everyone else
seems to muddle by
well enough
unfailingly okay
at everything they try to do
while I work so hard
just to break down
my own perfectionism enough
to open the Word document
& start typing.
Because when 'good enough'
is not good enough
mediocrity
is not
better than nothing.

FLIGHT: **NZ5627**
FROM: **HLZ** TO: **CHC**
DATE: **30OCT**

ESTIMATED
BOARDING: **13:20**PM

SEAT: **09B**
K001

Astronaut
They say never
to meet your heroes.
They say
you will be disappointed
when you learn they are
only human.
I say always
meet your heroes.
Write to the cool people.
Tell the amazing scientist
you're a big fan.
At the absolute worst,
in the humanity of your idol
you will see
the wonderful things
mere humans can do.

astronaut

They say never
to meet your heroes.
They say
you will be disappointed
when you learn they are
only human.
I say always
meet your heroes.
Write to the cool people.
Tell the amazing scientist
you're a big fan.
At the absolute worst,
in the humanity of your idol
you will see
the wonderful things
mere humans can do.

Terms & Conditions

I love
the You I know
in the time I know you.

I don't know if I would
love you differently [different person]
if you were a fundamentally
or if I had met you
at a very different time.

Suppose though
(hypothetically)
I knew everyone you
have ever been
will ever be
including the people you keep
in the secret corners of the mind.
If one could bring oneself
to love someone
one knew completely
(rather than the usual method
loving what one knows
& believing the best
about the rest
to the bitter end)
would that love be perfect
or merely
unconditional?

terms & conditions

I love
the You I know
in the time I know you.
I don't know if I would
love you differently
if you were a fundamentally different person,
or if I had met you
at a very different time.
Suppose though
(hypothetically)
I knew everyone you
have ever been
will ever be,
including the people you keep
in the secret corners of the mind.
If one could bring oneself
to love someone
one knew completely
(rather than the usual method:
loving what one knows
& believing the best
about the rest
to the bitter end)
would that love be perfect
or merely
unconditional?

Engineering Memory

I forgot about
the engineers
in writing about how I ∏
ended up being this person
doing these things
in the same way you forget about
the warp threads
in writing about
the symbolism on a tapestry.
I forgot about
the engineers
in the same way you forget
~~forgot~~ learning to speak your native Language
I forgot
that accounting for the width of
the tape-measure clip
checking that squares are square
fixing wiring yourself
designing structures in your head
are not part of
the default human software pack
Most of all, though,
I forgot about
the engineers
because in a long line
of second sons of second sons
who are all engineers
I did not recognize
the template of me.

engineering memory

I forgot about
the engineers
in writing about how I ended up
being this person,
doing these things,
the same way you forget about
the warp threads
in writing about
the symbolism on a tapestry.
I forgot about
the engineers
the same way you forget
learning to speak your native language.
I forgot
that accounting for the width of
the tape-measure clip,
checking that squares are square,
fixing wiring yourself,
designing structures in your head,
are not part of
the default human software pack.
Most of all, though,
I forgot about
the engineers
because in a long line
of second sons of second sons
who are all engineers
I did not recognize
the template of me.

[miTimend → Time mind]& v.v.
  it is that part of the year
 when the clock talks on
 but nobody is listening;
 when we all float by on
 the sickysweet red & green flood
 of CHRISTMAS
 corpses bloated with
 the guilt of knowing this is all
 supposed to be great fun
 weighed down with
 the stress of the year &
 the extra work of taking a break;
 when the days all have names
 that are not their real names
 & you go to church on a Tuesday;
 when breakfasttime is noon
 & this year
 the poor small hours of the night
 no longer exsist
 just when nothing else does either
 & we need them;
 the restless dog   [clock
 who demanded attention to the
 & walks under the stars
 & in the pearly chill of summer dawns
 is resting now.
 The nights are quiet
 The days are lost.
 There is no time & I am going
  out of my mind.

time out of mind, and vice versa

It is that part of the year
when the clock talks on
but nobody is listening;
when we all float by on
the sickly-sweet red-and-green flood
of CHRISTMAS,
corpses bloated with
the guilt of knowing this is all
supposed to be great fun,
weighed down with
the stress of the year &
the extra work of taking a break;
when the days all have names
that are not their real names,
& you go to church on a Tuesday;
when breakfasttime is noon.
& this year
the poor small hours of the night
no longer exist,
just when nothing else does either
& we needed them:
the restless dog
who demanded attention to the clock
& walks under the stars
& in the pearly chill of summer dawns
is resting now.
The nights are quiet.
The days are lost.
There is no time &
I am going
out of my mind.